World's Strangest "True" Ghost Stories

John Macklin

Illustrations by Elise Chanowitz

 Sterling Publishing Co., Inc.   New York

Library of Congress Cataloging-in-Publication Data

Macklin, John.
   [Strange and uncanny]
   World's strangest "true" ghost stories / John Macklin ;
illustrated by Elise Chanowitz.
      p.   cm.
   "Text . . . excerpted from the Strange and uncanny, © 1967"--T. p.
verso.
   Summary: A collection of twenty-three incidents involving
hauntings, jinxes, evil spirits, and other ghostly manifestations.
   1. Ghosts--Juvenile literature.   [1. Ghosts.]   I. Chanowitz,
Elise, ill.   II. Title.
BF1461.M339   1990   89-26125
133.1--dc20   CIP
                                        AC

10   9

First paperback edition published in 1991 by
Sterling Publishing Company, Inc.
387 Park Avenue South, New York, N.Y. 10016
Illustrations © 1990 by Elise Chanowitz
The text in this book has been excerpted
from *The Strange and Uncanny* © 1967 by Ace Books, Inc.
Distributed in Canada by Sterling Publishing
% Canadian Manda Group, P.O. Box 920, Station U
Toronto, Ontario, Canada M8Z 5P9
Distributed in Great Britain and Europe by Cassell PLC
Villiers House, 41/47 Strand, London WC2N 5JE, England
Distributed in Australia by Capricorn Ltd.
P.O. Box 665, Lane Cove, NSW 2066
Manufactured in the United States of America
All rights reserved

Sterling ISBN 0-8069-5784-0   Trade
                 0-8069-5785-9   Paper

CONTENTS

1. INCREDIBLE!

- A kitten appears in a photograph—three weeks after its death.

- A man is actually swallowed by a whale—and tells what it is like.

- A monk is seen flying through the air by dozens of witnesses.

- A horse reports accurately on the whereabouts of missing persons.

The Case of the Kitten Ghost

It lies in a special file in the Paris headquarters of the French Society for Psychical Research—a photograph of a small boy in his Sunday best, holding a pet kitten in his arms. The kitten is small and white with huge, appealing eyes set in a tiny face. It had been given to seven-year-old René Leret in August 1954, and from that moment on, the boy and the little cat were seldom apart.

René took the kitten to school—at least until the teacher objected. It slept on his bed, often sat on his knees at mealtimes.

"If anything happens to that cat, I dread to think what René would do," Michelle Leret remarked to her husband one night. "It would break the boy's heart."

But when that day came, there was no grief in the cottage on the edge of the village of Sampier, near Lyons in southeastern France. For it seemed that not even death could separate René Leret and his pet.

The events at Sampier, at first written off as a small child's fantasies, soon attracted the attention of France's top ghost hunters.

"I have studied well over 2,000 cases in the course of my career," wrote Dr. Gerard Lefeve of the French Society of Psychical Research, "and only five times have I failed to put the supernatural into natural terms. One of these was the case of the kitten at Sampier."

It was the first week of August in 1954 when René's uncle came to visit, bringing presents for everyone, including the tiny kitten for René. Immediately, the child christened it Jacques, and took it with him everywhere.

But the friendship—at least in normal terms—was to last only a month. One Saturday morning the kitten suddenly dashed through the garden into the main road. An oil truck on its way from Lyons to Dijon dashed the life from the tiny scrap of fur.

The parents kept the boy away from the scene until all traces of the accident were removed. "You must not be too sad about Jacques," Michelle Leret gently told her son. "We will get you another little kitten to take his place."

"I don't need another one, Mother," the boy replied. "Jacques is here sitting by the window." He reached out to stroke the air a few inches above the window ledge.

The parents regarded the action as a defense mechanism shielding René against the grief of losing his pet. Doubtless it would disappear in a couple of days.

But it didn't. Jacques had to have his food put out as usual; the door had to be opened to let him in; the cushion on which he had slept had to be in its place on René's bed.

One day, Charles Leret told his son gently but firmly that the pretense had gone on long enough. The child was bewildered: "But what do you mean? Jacques is here on the carpet—can't you see?"

The next day the worried parents called a doctor and told him their child was suffering from hallucinations. But examinations—culminating in hospital tests—could find nothing mentally wrong with the child.

Dr. Lefeve, hearing of the phenomenon, arrived at the village at the end of September. He had several long interviews with the child and his parents, and he carried out several routine tests. He found that when the child entered the room the temperature appeared to drop slightly—always a sign of a "presence."

Examining the inside of the front door, he found minute scratches around the bottom, apparently made by cat claws. Yet the door had been newly painted—after the cat had died.

Then there was the photograph. Dr. Lefeve was in the Leret house when it came back from the local pharmacy. The folder containing prints from a roll of film taken by Charles Leret was opened and the contents casually examined. There were pictures of the house, the family and the garden.

And there was a picture of René, taken near the garden gate. Charles Leret's hand shook as he handed the picture to the doctor. René, in his best clothes, looked strangely solemn. In his arms was a white kitten.

"The parents were astonished," Dr. Lefeve recalls. "When the photo was taken, there was no kitten or anything else in the child's arms. I examined the photograph and there was no doubt that the object was a kitten.

"I asked the parents every question I could think of and they answered willingly and honestly, but they could not throw any light on the mystery."

And no one ever has. For the picture of René Leret had been taken three weeks *after* Jacques the kitten had died.

Swallowed by a Whale— and He Lived!

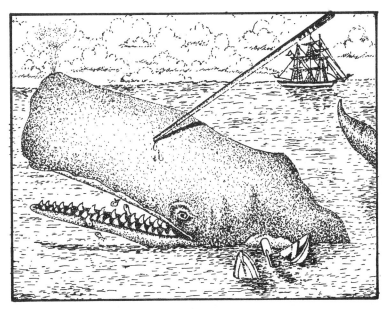

In the pale light of an Arctic summer afternoon, a boat was lowered from the deck of the whaling ship *Star of the East* and set out towards a school of sperm whales that was cruising nearby.

Thirty-five-year-old James Bartley was steering, six men were rowing, and another four were preparing harpoons. Behind them, *Star of the East* edged in to pick up the whales they caught.

It was to be the last short trip before the whaler, stocked with blubber, sailed for England. The 1891 season had been her most successful. And it was to be capped by one of the most incredible experiences in the history of the sea.

So improbable did the incident seem that the captain and the entire crew of *Star of the East* later thought it necessary to tell under oath how James Bartley was *swallowed by a whale.*

By late afternoon the harpoon team had killed one whale and wounded another. Bartley steered towards the wounded whale and three men prepared to spear it again.

Suddenly the whale turned. Seizing the prow of the boat in its jaws, it shook it the way a dog shakes a bone, splitting the vessel in half.

The sailors dived into the water and were picked up by another boat from *Star of the East.* James Bartley was the last to jump. As he leaped over the stern, the whale made a quick turn in the water, opened its mouth and caught him. The huge jaws closed tightly over the man.

The next day, a dead whale floated to the surface of the ocean, a harpoon stuck in its side. The whale was hauled aboard *Star of the East*, and for two days the men worked to remove its blubber.

When the job was finished, it occurred to one of the sailors that the only whale that had been harpooned and not caught during recent trips was the one that had eaten Bartley.

The men decided to cut up the whale. As they opened the stomach, to their amazement and horror the outline of a man showed through the tissue. Carefully slicing the muscles away, they uncovered the missing sailor, unconscious but still alive!

Carefully they got the man out and placed him on the deck, rubbing his limbs and forcing brandy down his throat. Working on him in relays, the sailors slowly restored his circulation and Bartley recovered at least partial consciousness.

He seemed delirious and repeatedly cried out that he was "in a fiery furnace." After several days he recovered. By the time the ship returned to England he was able to make a statement about his terrible experience. This is what he said:

"I remember very well from the moment I jumped from the boat and felt my feet strike some soft substance.

"I looked up and saw a big-ribbed canopy of light pink and white descending over me, and the next moment I felt myself being drawn downwards, feet first. I realized I was being swallowed by a whale.

"I was drawn lower and lower, a wall of flesh surrounding me and hemming me in on every side, yet the pressure was not painful and the flesh easily gave way before my slightest movement.

"Suddenly I found myself in a sack much larger than my body, but completely dark. I felt about me and my hand came in contact with several fishes, some of which seemed to be still alive because they squirmed in my fingers and slipped back to my feet. Soon I felt a great pain in the head and breathing became more and more difficult. At the same time, I felt a terrible heat, and it seemed to consume me, growing hotter and hotter.

"My eyes became coals of fire in my head. I believed every minute that I was about to die.

"There was an awful silence in my prison. I tried to rise, to move my arms and legs, to cry out. All action was now impossible but my brain was abnormally clear, and with a full comprehension of my awful fate, I finally lost consciousness."

The only lasting effect of the experience seems to have been a recurring nightmare in which he relived the sensations he felt in the whale's stomach. After his recovery, Bartley returned to sea and died in 1926 at the age of 65.

The whole crew of the whaler gave their testimony on oath before a Justice of the Peace.

Even so, M. Henri de Parville, scientific editor of the Paris magazine *Journal des Debats*, debated for four and a half years whether to publish the facts in his possession. Every item was checked and rechecked. Bartley was interviewed privately and his story compared with those of his companions. Finally convinced of the truth, de Parville published the story.

Bartley became a celebrity. Doctors discovered he had an extraordinarily strong constitution. Even so, to remain alive for nearly three days in a virtually airless prison made medical history.

Bartley just failed to equal Jonah's feat centuries before. The Bible records that Jonah was in full possession of his faculties for four days while inside the whale.

The Flying Monk

This question has baffled churchmen and scholars for nearly 300 years: Could St. Joseph of Copertino fly in the air?

The incredible exploits of this 17th century Italian monk were seen and vouched for by nearly 100 witnesses—including a pope. And the written accounts of his flights give absolutely no clue to how they were done. Had he actually discovered the secret of how to overcome gravity?

By any standards, St. Joseph was an extraordinary man. From the age of 12 he wore a hair shirt next to his skin and a heavy iron chain drawn tightly around his waist. Frequently he fasted for long periods. As he grew older he became even more serious and strict. By the time he joined the Order of St. Francis in 1625 he was no longer content just to wear an iron chain about his waist. He attached a large metal plate to it, which tore at his body.

Stories began to circulate that he possessed supernatural powers. These tales became so widespread that he was ordered to Naples for questioning by the Holy Office. He was examined three times. The fourth time, he begged to be allowed to say Mass in the Inquisition's own church of St. Gregory of Armenia. After the ceremony, Joseph knelt to pray. A few moments later, startled onlookers were hardly able to believe their eyes.

Rising in the air, Joseph floated over the amazed congregation. Then he flew to the altar and alighted amid the flowers and burning candles.

Nuns who were present called out: "The candles! The candles—he'll catch fire!"

But Joseph robes did not catch fire, although the flames from the candles licked them several times. After a few minutes, he rose into the air again and flew back into the body of the church.

The court of the Inquisition rushed him off to Rome to have an audience with the Pope.

As he entered into the presence of the Pontiff and before a word had been spoken, Joseph drifted up into the air and remained suspended for fully a minute.

Later, Joseph was sent to a monastery in Assisi. One Christmas Eve, a party of shepherds was invited to his church to play music upon their pipes. They had barely started when Joseph "began to dance and suddenly he gave a great sigh and flew like an angel onto the High Altar." He remained there for about 20 minutes, again in the midst of flaming candles. Then he flew down again and blessed the shepherds.

On another occasion, Joseph was walking with the priest Antonio Chiarello when he suddenly flew across the garden in which they were walking and came to rest on top of an olive tree. Chiarello was amazed to see that the branch that bore Joseph's weight was hardly as thick as a man's finger.

Not content with "solo flights," Joseph began to take other people with him. His first "passenger" was the father confessor of the Convent of Santa Chiara in Copertino. During a festival, Joseph grasped his fellow-priest by the hand and rose up with him into the air.

One of the most extraordinary demonstrations of Joseph's strange gift occurred when he came upon ten laborers who had collapsed exhausted upon the ground after hauling a huge cross of solid walnut.

Joseph asked, "What is the matter, my children?" The men explained that they were so tired that they found it completely impossible to drag the great cross the last yards to the spot on the crest of a hill where they had to erect it.

The monk took off his cloak and ordered them to stand aside. "I am here!" he cried, rushing towards the cross.

Then, as though it weighed only a few pounds, he flew with the cross, carrying it right over their heads, and set it down in the hole that had been prepared for it.

Even on his deathbed, on September 17th, 1663, Joseph amazed everyone—including his doctors—by rising from the bed and flying as far as the little chapel of the monastery.

The story of his ability to fly was vouched for scores of times, by the most eminent and respectable of witnesses. All were satisfied that he used no mechanical tricks.

Joseph went to his grave taking his secret with him.

The Psychic Horse

The two men could barely keep a straight face as the stable door opened and out shuffled the oldest, boniest horse they had ever seen. This clinched it! Now there was no mistake: The whole thing was a hoax.

On the face of it, the feelings of the men who stood in the stable yard in St. John's, Newfoundland, Canada, in October, 1955, would have been echoed by anyone with normal healthy skepticism.

For they had been persuaded, despite their better judgment, to seek advice from this pathetic creature on the fate of a missing child.

But within minutes, what appeared to be a joke in rather bad taste was transformed into an uncanny glimpse into the supernatural that no one has ever been able to explain.

It soon became obvious that only one being in the whole of Canada knew what had happened to three-year-old Ronnie Weitcamp. And that was Lady Wonder, a 30-year-old mare, spending the twilight of its days in a stable a hundred miles away.

On October 11, 1955, Ronnie left his three playmates in the front yard of his home near a Newfoundland naval base, and ran around to the back of the house. He disappeared into some nearby woods and, despite the pleas of his playmates, wouldn't come out. As they ran to tell his mother, the child roamed deeper into the woods.

Neighbors scoured the woodland. By mid-afternoon, the police had been called and a full-scale search mounted. As darkness fell, 1,500 searchers combed bushes and ravines. The bitter cold descended. They knew that if the child was not found, there was little chance of his surviving the night.

But he wasn't found, and the police, convinced that their search had been thorough, turned to other theories: Had he been kidnapped?

Eleven days passed, and there was no sign of the child. The tips and leads supplied by the public led to nothing and hope was finally abandoned.

Then a police official remembered that, years before, a child had been found through information supplied by a horse!

In any other circumstances it would have been laughable, but the police looking for little Ronnie Weitcamp had become desperate. Eventually, when hope was nearly extinguished, two detectives were sent to interview the horse.

By any standards, Lady Wonder was a remarkable horse. By the time she was two years old she had learned to count and spell out words by moving children's blocks around. One day she spelled out "engine" as a huge tractor rumbled past the house. Later, in response to questions, the horse would use her nose to flip up large tin letters that hung from a bar across her stall. In this way, she spelled out the answers to questions put to her.

The fame of the horse had spread. Thousands came to seek answers to their queries. She was claimed to have predicted that Franklin D. Roosevelt would be the next president of the United States, before he had even been nominated.

She picked the winners of countless races, and venturing into the field of mathematics, briskly calculated the cube roots of numbers. University specialists in extrasensory perception spent weeks testing the horse, and came away convinced that she had some kind of telepathic powers.

But she remained basically a harmless curiosity until one day police, after a four-month search for a seven-year-old girl, turned in desperation to Lady Wonder. She directed them to a water-filled quarry that already had been searched without success. A further hunt led to the child's body, exactly where the horse had indicated.

Coincidence or not, in the absence of any other idea it was worth trying. But now the horse was old and such tests upset her. After convincing the owner this was an emergency, the officers were eventually allowed to question Lady Wonder.

The bar of letters was put in place and the questions

began. They asked: "Do you know why we are here?" Immediately the horse spelled out: "Boy."

Q: Do you know the boy's name?

A: Ronnie.

Q: Is he dead or alive?

A: Dead.

Q: Was he kidnapped?

A: No.

Q: Will he be found?

A: Yes.

Q: Where?

A: Hole.

Q: What is near him?

A: Elm.

Q: What kind of soil?

A: Sand.

Q: When will he be found?

A: December.

That was the end of the interview. Refusing to answer any further questions, the mare tottered away. The detectives telephoned headquarters with the answers and a new search was discussed.

A storm of ridicule descended as it became known the police were acting on the advice of a horse. Naval base officials, particularly, insisted that the ground had been thoroughly searched and it was quite obvious that the child had been abducted. However, a new search took place, nothing was found, and the police department began to curse the day they sought the help of Lady Wonder.

Then on the afternoon of Sunday, December 4, the body of Ronnie Weitcamp was found by two boys in a thicket at the bottom of a ravine about a mile from his home. He had not been kidnapped: Medical evidence showed he had died of exposure. He lay in sandy soil, just out of the shade of the nearest tree—a large elm.

Every detail of the horse's prediction had been proved uncannily accurate; it was unbelievable but true. It was also the last time Lady Wonder used the swinging letters.

The following spring, she died, taking with her the mystery of her glimpses into a world few humans have ever penetrated.

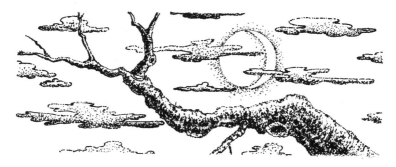

2. BACK FROM THE DEAD

- A man gets off a train and waves to his friends at the same moment that his body is lying dead in a hospital miles away.

- A captain saves the lives of 74 members of his crew—while floating lifeless in the sea.

- A boy is miraculously saved from drowning by his father—who was drowned himself years before.

The Weekend Guest Who Wasn't There

It was on a June morning in 1936 that Dr. John Rowley received a letter that triggered off the strangest episode of his life.

It came from Arthur Sherwood, a former medical school colleague practising in London.

"Thank you for your invitation for a long weekend," he wrote. "A spell in the country would doubtless do me the world of good. I will travel by the 10:30 train on Friday."

So it was that Dr. Rowley, a middle-aged bachelor in general practice in a rural district in England's West Country became involved in one of the most curious and inexplicable stories of the century.

On the day of his friend's arrival, Dr. Rowley had an early lunch and set off for Exeter to meet the London train. Passing a bus stop in his car, he noticed a friend, a middle-aged architect, and stopped to give him a lift. As the station was some distance from the center of town, Dr. Rowley invited his friend to meet the train with him; afterwards, he would make a small detour and drop him off at his office.

The architect agreed. They arrived at the station five minutes before the train was due and parked the car. Then they walked up to the bridge that spanned the tracks and leaned over it, so they had a complete view of the platform at which the train would arrive.

The train was three minutes early, and only four passengers got off: three men and a girl. One of the men was Dr. Sherwood. "That's him," Dr. Rowley said, pointing to a thickset man in a raincoat and bowler hat.

Dr. Rowley shouted down a greeting. The man looked up, waved and smiled; then, picking up his suitcase, he hurried out of sight towards the station exit.

Dr. Rowley and his companion walked down to meet him. The other men and the girl came out, but there was no sign of Dr. Sherwood.

"Did the man in the bowler hat already go through?" Dr. Rowley asked the ticket collector. "Only three people got off the train," he replied. "And they have come through." He held out, as proof, three tickets.

Both the doctor and his companion protested that there was a mistake. They were allowed through the barrier and searched the station buildings for over half an hour, but found no one.

Disturbed and bewildered, Dr. Rowley returned home. He had been in the house just a few minutes when a telegram arrived. It was from Dr. Sherwood's partner in London. It reported that Dr. Sherwood had been fatally injured that morning in a street accident soon after leaving his home for his weekend in the country.

A telephone call confirmed that this was true. Dr. Sherwood had been knocked down by a taxi and taken, unconscious, to a hospital, where he died as the result of a fractured skull.

What possible explanation could there be? Later, at the request of Dr. Rowley, Francis Grafton, the architect who had accompanied him to the station, wrote the following statement: "It was nearly 10:30 A.M. when I accompanied the doctor to the railway station. The sun was out and the light extremely good. We were standing on the bridge waiting for the train, barely 50 yards from the platform.

"Four passengers definitely alighted from the train—three men and a woman. Of this, I am quite sure.

"The eldest passenger was a man wearing a bowler hat and carrying a case. Dr. Rowley pointed him out to me as the man he had come to meet. When Dr. Rowley hailed him, the passenger smiled and waved.

"When we got to the barrier, only three people were waiting to come through.

"I am of a skeptical nature, and do not believe in ghosts. Nevertheless, I am completely unable to give any rational explanation for the incident. I confess it is an utter mystery to me."

Is there an explanation?

Psychic researchers call this type of ghost a "subjective" phantom. They suggest that it is a hybrid being, created by the disembodied spirit of the dead person combining with some "piece of matter" to produce a temporary, though very elementary, intelligence.

Other authorities insist that this sort of ghost is a timeless "thought-form" produced by people of the past, present and future—an image of another world that becomes perceptible to certain people under special conditions.

This, say the experts, was probably what was seen by the men on the bridge—the image of a man who had slipped temporarily into another dimension of time and space.

You may not agree with this explanation. But can you think of any other?

The Phantom Captain

He was a tall, broad-shouldered man with a barrel chest and an unmistakable air of command. A vivid scar curved across his temple and down his left cheek.

The men in the wheelhouse of the three-masted ship, the *James Gilbert*, beating through monstrous waves on the 4,600 mile run from Cape of Good Hope to Bombay that January night in 1902, all saw him clearly. They felt the blast of spray as he forced open the wheelhouse door and spoke to them as they struggled with the buffetting wheel.

The orders given by this man with captain's rings on his sleeve saved the lives of 74 men who were within a few hours of a hideous death from starvation and exposure.

Yet, at that very moment, the body of this man was floating lifeless on the storm-tossed waters of the Indian Ocean. Of this there is no doubt.

Nor is there any doubt that the story of the phantom captain is one of the strangest and best documented of all inexplicable tales of the sea, still often discussed when sailors gather to swap yarns.

The *James Gilbert* was 40 years old when she sailed into marine history. Her square rig and jaunty profile made her a picture-book ship, and, when conditions were right, she could still outrun most of the new-fangled steamships on the routes.

In the midwinter of 1902, the *James Gilbert* left London with 68 officers and crew and 15 passengers bound for Bombay. Captain Frank Carter was in command. In a heavy overcoat, he patrolled the poop deck in the bleak evening air, as the vessel, a pilot at the helm, slipped downriver towards the sea. At Barking Creek, she dropped anchor. Chandlers' longboats came alongside with stores, including live poultry and a dozen live sheep, which were quartered in accommodations near the mainmast.

Dawn saw the *James Gilbert* out in the English Channel, heading west. With a tail wind, good weather and calm seas, she made excellent time sailing down the coast of Africa.

She rounded the Cape of Good Hope and veered northeast on the 4,600 mile last lap to Bombay. Six days later, the barometer fell with alarming speed and within a few hours the wind had reached gale force. Waves were crashing over the decks. Cabins were flooded and passengers huddled in the crew's quarters. A wall of water smashed into the galley, reducing it to chaos. Sails ripped and ropes chafed until they snapped.

On the orders of the captain, oil bags were hauled out

of the main hatch and punctured so that their contents would smooth the water. But the waves were too violent for the oil to have much effect.

For 48 hours, Captain Carter never left the wheelhouse. Two men and sometimes three were needed to keep the ship on course. Up in the rigging, men risked their lives to shorten the sail that was tearing loose from its lashings.

On the morning of the second day, the storm eased enough to allow the crew to begin clearing up the wreckage. Then it blew again, but with less ferocity, and Captain Carter, leaving the second mate in charge, went below for a few hours' sleep.

In the wheelhouse during the middle watch was the helmsman, assisted by a seaman and an apprentice. The second mate was on the poop deck, supervising a change of sail.

The helmsman, steering the northeasterly course ordered by Captain Carter, was complaining about the quality of the officers aboard when the apprentice nudged his arm. "Pipe down," he said, "we've got a visitor."

A tall, stocky man in a captain's uniform pushed into the cramped wheelhouse past the astonished helmsman and peered into the compass.

The binnacle light revealed a long and livid scar running almost the length of his face. Without looking up, the stranger said, "Steer nor' nor' east."

"I'm not taking any orders except the captain's," said the helmsman, "and he said nor' east."

"I said nor' nor' east," the man said angrily, "and look lively, for every moment counts." Then he opened the door and disappeared onto the deck.

The helmsman didn't know what to do. Should he take the order? The second mate was still out on deck. Perhaps the man was travelling as a passenger, and simply transmitting an order from the captain.

Satisfied with this explanation, the helmsman spun the wheel. The ship swung slowly onto a fresh course.

Captain Carter woke in the early dawn to excited shouting from the deck. He found his crew hurling out ropes to the occupants of four battered lifeboats tossing in the heavy swell on the port side of the ship.

The boats were secured and more than 70 men in an advanced state of exhaustion and shock clambered up the sides of the *James Gilbert.*

One of them explained: "We're from the brig *Firebird,* sir. The ship caught fire two days ago. She burned down to the waterline and then went down. You showed up just in time—we couldn't have lasted another hour."

"Is your captain here?" Captain Carter asked.

"No, sir," replied the sailor. "He was killed as we lowered our boats. The mainmast came down and struck him a fatal blow across the head. He was our only fatality."

The survivors went below for food and medical treatment and the ship continued on her original course. An hour later, a lookout sighted an object on the starboard bow.

It was the body of a man, a broad-shouldered man with a barrel chest and a vivid scar down the left of his face. He wore captain's rings on his uniform sleeve.

Death at the Falls

There is a long slim gravestone on the American side of Niagara Falls commemorating those who met their deaths in the raging whirlpool below the falling cliffs of water.

Some died by accident. Others flung themselves over the falls for fame or money. For others it was a way out of black despair.

A few of them lived for a little while. But Patrick Neil Thompson was not among that elite band. He fell over Niagara Falls one winter night in 1940 and was never seen again—at least not alive.

But how he reappeared two years later, when his son Kenneth was beyond any human aid, is a story that people who live and work within the thunder of the Falls still remember and tell.

Patrick Thompson was a civil engineer. He lived with

his wife and son in the small village of Hampstone on the Canadian side of Niagara Falls.

In the late 1930s, the Rainbow Bridge, an old suspension bridge connecting the American and Canadian shores some miles up the Niagara River, had been swept away by ice packs.

The company that employed Thompson won the major contract to build a new one.

Construction started early in 1939. It was priority work. The Canadians would soon be at war and every bridge was needed. The men were working in shifts around the clock to replace the Rainbow Bridge. Patrick Thompson was in charge of a team of ten men who were working nights under floodlights on a scaffolded platform in the middle of the Niagara River.

On the night of January 17, 1940, Thompson was supervising concrete being unloaded from a barge into a hopper on the rig. A wind of almost gale force was lashing up from Lake Erie, building the waves on the Niagara River into what looked like oceanic proportions. The string of barges in the darkness below banged and rattled against the rig. Thompson stood guiding the crane bucket into the hopper.

Suddenly, the wind caught the crane jib and whipped it savagely to the right. The bucket, at about chest height, caught Thompson, knocking him off the platform into the churning water below.

Five miles downstream the Falls were waiting.

He must have been unconscious or semiconscious from the blow because they heard no sound. Boats were sent out and searchlights raked the water, but Patrick Thompson was never seen again.

An inquest returned a verdict of death by drowning. The Coroner expressed sympathy for his widow and son. The company said they were sorry to lose such a fine man.

Patrick Thompson died the day before his birthday. He would have been 32 years old.

Doris Thompson went back to Hampstone and took a job in the office of a building firm. Her son Kenneth, now ten, was going to the local school.

Two years went by. Mother and son were surviving and it looked as though they were recovering pretty well from the blow fate had dealt them.

But fate, it seemed, had not yet done with the Thompson family. In the first week of April 1942, Kenneth and two friends were on the bank of the Niagara River. The spring thaw had swollen it into a mile-wide torrent. The boys watched as huge uprooted trees lurched past in the grip of the relentless current. They threw small branches into the water and saw them scud away towards the distant roar of the Falls.

Suddenly, Kenneth Thompson, overwhelmed by enthusiasm for the game, grasped a large bough and tossed it over the bank. With a scream, he lost his balance and toppled into the stream. His two friends watched transfixed as the boy was whirled away.

Incredibly, he did not drown: He clung to the branch, which, bobbing and rearing like a macabre steed, swept him steadily towards the Falls and destruction. His friends, shocked into action, ran to their bicycles and made for the nearest telephone.

The boatmen at Horseshoe Falls prepared their rescue vessels and lifelines but they knew it was hopeless.

Water at least 40 feet thick was hurling itself over the 400-foot-high curve of rock. Spray lashed hundreds of feet into the air. No human life could persist amid such fury.

Kenneth, on the last bend before the Falls, felt the branch on which he rode speed up like a powerful car. He struggled to keep his head above water. His numb fingers slipped off the bark, and the branch jerked free of him.

As Kenneth sank deeply into the blinding waters, he felt in his heart that he would never rise again. Straight ahead, he could see the semicircular outline of the edge of the Falls and knew the end was only seconds away.

Then it happened. He felt arms closing around his shoulders. No longer was he drifting helplessly on the current. He could feel the water surging against him, but he was no longer moving. Firmly held by some unknown, unseen force, he began to move towards the bank.

Then he heard the voice. It was low, soft, and heartbreakingly familiar. It said: "Hold on to me and don't be afraid. I will take care of you."

It was the voice of his father. Of that, Kenneth Thompson had no doubt. Nor had he any doubt that some tangible presence supported him on that 100-yard fight against the current, and helped him up the bank to safety.

Because Kenneth Thompson could not swim.

3. HAUNTED PLACES

- The famous palace at Versailles— haunted by its past—or did the schoolteachers who visited it step into a loop in time?

- A stretch of road that has continual accidents—could they have been caused by a phantom truck?

- Strange voices sing archaic Latin Masses—and only the children hear them.

- An abandoned house is still "lived in" by a tragic family.

They Walked into the Past

When people talk about time travel, one story is quoted more than any other. It is, perhaps, the most astonishing and well-documented ghost story of all.

It was on a summer's day in 1901 that two women visitors to France's Palace of Versailles travelled back 200 years in time—to the spacious, leisurely days of the 18th century.

They saw buildings that had been demolished generations before, watched people strolling about in clothes they had previously seen only in museums—and saw Marie Antoinette sketching on the lawn!

There is no rational explanation for the strange experiences of Anne Moberly, Principal of St. Hugh's College, Oxford, and her friend, Eleanor Jourdain, the college's lecturer in French, which took place during a vacation they spent together in France.

Near the end of their trip, while visiting Versailles, they went looking for the Petit Trianon, Marie Antoinette's summer home. Having only a small guidebook map, they didn't notice the deserted drive that would have led to their destination, and they got lost.

Following a narrow lane, they found themselves walking through thickly wooded glades that led to a group of farm buildings.

Accounts that both women later compiled showed that at the time both of them noticed an eerie stillness in the air.

They asked their way of two men, dressed in long, greyish green coats. Because of a wheelbarrow and a spade nearby, the women assumed that the men were gardeners. "We did not realize at the time," wrote Miss Jourdain later, "that the style of their dress was at least 200 years old."

Miss Jourdain noticed a woman and a girl standing at the stone steps of a cottage. That was to prove a most significant detail.

Even when, a little later, the women met a man wearing a wide-brimmed hat and cloak that would only have been worn at a fancy dress ball, the incident still did not strike them as odd!

This man had a pockmarked face and an extremely dark complexion. Both women felt frightened by him. They were greatly relieved when another man ran up to them crying: "May I show you the way, mesdames?"

He indicated a small bridge over a ravine. Presently,

they arrived at a clearing in front of the Petit Trianon. On a stool, a woman sat sketching.

Once again, the teachers noticed that curious air of oppressiveness. And, once again, it seemed that some alien agent had willed them to disregard the fact that everyone they saw was dressed almost 200 years behind the times.

It was only after the two women returned to Paris that they began comparing notes. Then they realized they had each seen things that the other hadn't.

Miss Moberly said it was a pity that they hadn't spoken to the woman who was sketching, only for her friend to deny having seen such a woman.

Similarly, Miss Moberly had not seen the woman and the girl seen by her friend.

Three months later, Miss Jourdain made a second trip to the Petit Trianon. The joyful sound of music drifted across the park and she noted the tune that was being played. She also saw two laborers in red and blue capes filling a cart with sticks.

She was shattered when the caretaker of the Petit Trianon told her that no band had played that day and also laughed at her story of having seen men in red and blue capes. "Such capes haven't been worn for 200 years," he told the astonished woman.

A few weeks later, both teachers made another pilgrimage to Versailles together. Many of the landmarks that they had both seen the first time were gone.

It became clear to them that, in some way they could not explain, they had been given a glimpse of Versailles as it was in Marie Antoinette's day.

In the archives of the French Academy of History,

Miss Moberly found some proof to support this incredible theory. The grey-green costume they had seen proved to have been the old royal livery. Two brothers in this garb had always been on duty near the cottage when the Queen was in residence.

The cottage Miss Jourdain had noticed where the woman and a girl stood was identified on an old engraving. Records showed that in 1789 a 14-year-old girl and her mother had lived there.

A kiosk that both had seen was found in a map of 1783. And at that time, the Queen's intimate friends had included a Comte de Vaudreuil—a pockmarked Creole, who often wore a large cloak and Spanish hat.

The music Miss Jourdain heard proved to have been a tune of the period around 1780.

The two friends inspected pictures of Marie Antoinette. One of them was very much like the sketching woman that Miss Moberly had seen.

They could not trace the bridge and ravine they had crossed until, in 1913, an old map was found stuffed up a chimney. Drawn in the hand of Marie Antoinette's landscape gardener, it clearly showed the bridge and ravine.

Many people now believe that in some mysterious way, the women had been transported into the past— but why?

"I would not have believed such a thing could happen, had I read it or been told of it," Miss Moberly wrote, "but now I know that indeed all things are possible."

The Ghost Truck

Just before midnight on a February night in 1930, a group of men gathered by the side of a lonely lane in northwest England. The men were members of a coroner's jury. They had come out to this desolate spot—to seek out a ghost.

Earlier in the month, two men on a motorcycle had crashed in very mysterious circumstances on this same road. The driver had died, but his passenger had lived to tell the tale.

At the inquest, the passenger insisted that they had had to swerve violently on the night in question because a truck had suddenly backed out of an opening right across their path.

Yet police had inspected the stretch of road—and found there was no opening of any kind in the area from which a truck could have emerged.

"But I saw it as plain as can be!" burst in the passenger at the inquest.

"It was probably some form of optical illusion," the Coroner commented, but the passenger wouldn't accept the idea.

"There is an opening there. I'll show it to you," he insisted.

"In view of the great number of accidents that have taken place on that particular stretch of road during the past 22 months, I think it would be as well if this jury were to examine the scene of the mishap," the Coroner declared. "So far, no satisfactory explanation for any of these accidents has been forthcoming, and I think it is time the mystery was solved."

Because every one of the accidents had taken place at night, the Coroner added that it might be best if they visited the spot at "the witching hour."

"If there really is a phantom truck, then it should, according to ghost lore, appear at midnight," he concluded with a smile.

Altogether three people had been killed and an additional 25 injured at the spot in question. Eighteen cars had been involved in crashes, most of the drivers swearing that a vehicle of some sort had suddenly materialized across their path, seemingly from thin air.

Local residents were firmly convinced that a phantom vehicle was to blame. There were ghost ships, phantom armies and haunted coaches—why not a ghost truck?

"There are ghosts in these parts," they told the reporters. "You can hear them marching up and down the street at night. But when you go to look out of the window, there's nobody there.

"What's more, you can't get a dog to walk along that stretch of road at night. They can see something which sets them howling in terror."

The owner of a pub in the neighborhood went further and declared that every time the ghost walked, an accident took place. "There's no mistaking the tread," he told newspapermen. "It sounds like a very big man clumping along. I've heard it in the courtyard quite often—always late at night and at full moon. And then without fail somebody is found either dead or dying the next morning on the road."

And so, at midnight, February 18, 1930, the motorcycle passenger led the jury to the scene of the accident. Try though he might, however, he could not discover an opening of any sort.

"I can't understand it," he muttered, completely bewildered. "We both saw it backing out of this lane, or whatever it was."

"It was probably a patch of mist," remarked one of the jury members.

"This hedge and the wall adjoining caught in the sudden glare of a headlight could very well be mistaken for the back of a truck," ventured another.

The ghost truck did not put in an appearance that night, but soon afterwards a huge trailer truck went off the road at the exact same spot.

A few nights after that, a motorcyclist thought he saw something blocking the road ahead. He braked sharply and went careening into the hedge.

And so it went. A member of the Society for Psychical Research spent an entire night by the side of the road, but the phantom eluded him.

Police were convinced that the wall and the hedge were to blame and had them removed in due course. The accidents became less frequent, but they do still occasionally happen.

And it still takes a brave—or unimaginative—person to walk down that lonely lane at midnight when the moon is high. . . .

Voices of the Dead

On a warm summer evening in 1949, the four children of Captain and Mrs. Roland Macey finished their high tea in the panelled dining room of Fresden Priory, a rambling mansion that had once been a monastery.

They ran through the French windows and out onto a small flagged terrace where their mother was sitting with the local priest.

"Mother," said the oldest child, Mary, aged 12, "can we go upstairs and listen to the singing?"

"What is that?" the priest inquired.

"Oh," said the mother, "they say they can hear singing up in the nursery, but of course it is all nonsense."

It turned out that what the Macey children could hear was anything but nonsense. It was what psychic researchers call a "mass echo in time," and certainly the most uncanny and well documented example of "voices from the dead" ever reported.

For years, authorities on the occult had sought proof for the centuries-old belief that antique furniture or wooden altars used for Mass had the power to transmit through time the Latin chanting of monks who lived hundreds of years before.

Now, it seemed, the four Macey children were going to provide it.

The priest asked permission to accompany the children up to the nursery. There he saw a large table standing against a wall. The children stood beside the table and immediately became completely absorbed, although the priest could hear nothing. He asked them to try and sing along with what they called the "funny music," and they did.

When he returned downstairs, the priest told Mrs. Macey: "What your children can hear, but we cannot, is the monks who lived here 500 years ago, singing their evening office. It is archaic plain-chant Latin, completely unused today."

The children knew no Latin, were not Roman Catholic, and had never even heard a Latin Mass. So when they repeated what they heard "the table singing," there was no way to doubt them.

But children, it seemed, were the only ones privileged to hear the chanting monks. A team of experts arrived with high-frequency recording equipment and heard nothing.

The table itself was examined and later carefully taken apart. Underneath the false top was a wooden frame with a stone cross set in it. It was an altar used for secret Masses when Catholicism was illegal in England.

Dr. William Byrne, a medical student with a fine reputation as a psychic investigator, heard about the singing. He asked—and was granted—permission to visit the house.

Once again, the children repeated the words that they heard coming from the table. Some teenage cousins visiting the house claimed they could hear the singing too.

Late one evening, Dr. Byrne and two assistants, after making a series of unsuccessful tests in the house, were walking across the drive to their car when they became the first—and last—adults to hear for themselves the voices of the dead.

"We heard," Dr. Byrne was to explain later, "the sweet singing of ghostly monks. It was so clear on the air that I thought at first it was a radio turned on—but it was not. Then I realized we were below the window of the room in which the altar stood.

"For over half an hour, the chanting continued. Almost afraid to move, I reached out to switch on a portable tape recorder I was carrying.

"Suddenly the singing stopped. Then came slow reading by a man's voice. It came from the thin air about 20 feet from me. It was in some archaic form of Latin."

Then there was silence. Dr. Byrne clicked off his recorder and wound back the tape. Silently, the spools revolved—and only a quiet hiss emerged from the speaker.

The voices were, it seems, beyond the range of any man-made equipment.

How *can* the past be transmitted to us through inanimate objects?

Roger Pater, a well known expert on the occult, explains it like this: "Anything that has played a part in events that aroused very intense emotional activity seems to become itself saturated, as it were, with the emotions involved—so much so, that it can influence people of exceptional sympathetic powers, and enable them to see or hear the original events almost as though they had been there."

Is this the explanation for the phantom voices of Fresden Priory? It probably is—at least until someone can think of something better!

House for Sale

"Drive a little slower, dear," Therese Storrer said to her husband. "There's a house for sale."

Hans-Peter Storrer stepped on the brake, and the car slowed down, its spoked wheels brushing the roadside grass.

It was July 1908, and Therese and Hans-Peter Storrer were on the threshold of the strangest and most unaccountable experience of their lives. They were about to negotiate for a home of their own—with a family of ghosts.

The story of the Storrers, which unfolded in a village in the hills outside Vienna, has become a classic of Austrian psychic research. "Of all my investigations, this is the only case for which I can offer absolutely no rational explanation," wrote Dr. Paul Bonvin, a famous investigator of supernatural phenomena who died in 1925.

As the car coasted to a halt, Hans-Peter, a 28-year-old bank official, pushed up his dark glasses and examined the dusty "For Sale" notice.

The couple had been married for two years and had spent all that time living in the cramped flat of Therese's parents. They were searching anxiously for a house of their own, preferably in the country but reasonably near Vienna.

Hans-Peter swung the car around and started slowly up the narrow lane towards a house standing high above them on green sloping ground. As he drove, he noticed how grassed over and lacking in recent wheel marks the lane was.

The observation meant little to him at that moment. Later it slipped starkly, logically into place. For dead men don't drive cars.

A few minutes later, they reached a set of open iron gates leading onto a weedy courtyard. The house, in pale flaking brick, stood across an overgrown lawn. It was neglected; its paint was peeling. But there was no doubt that it had been an elegant house.

Hans-Peter stopped the car and helped his wife out. They waited a few moments but no one came to the door; no faces appeared at the window.

There was a curious oppressed silence that the couple broke with their footsteps as they walked towards the front door.

Later, Therese recalled what happened next. "We stood at the door, and Hans-Peter knocked. We heard the knocks resounding through the house—an eerie sound—but no one answered. There were curtains at the windows, and there appeared to be furniture inside.

We were quite sure the house was inhabited.

"Eventually, my husband tried the door. It was unlocked. There seemed little harm in having a quick look around now that we had gone this far. He went in first and I followed."

The house was dim and filled with cobwebs. The furnishings that filled every room were thick with dust, riddled with the ravages of moth and worm. In the kitchen, crockery and cutlery were laid out on a table for a meal that obviously had never been served. In the pantry, bread and vegetables, laid on the marble slabs, had long since rotted away.

All the trappings of living were there in the decaying, neglected house. Only the people were missing.

Therese resumed the story. "By this time I was ready to leave—I wouldn't have lived there however reasonable the price. But Hans-Peter was determined to look over the rest of the place.

"We walked along a gloomy corridor and opened a door to what I assumed to be the main living room of the house. The door swung back and we both saw them clearly. There *were* people in the house.

"Heavy curtains hung at the windows but there was still enough light for me to be certain of what I saw. There were four people in the room—a man, a woman, and two children. They were sitting immovably in chairs around the fireplace. It was like a weird tableau.

"After what seemed like hours—it could only have been seconds—they turned and looked at us. They were wearing clothes in vogue in the 1890s and the man held a silver-topped cane.

"Strangely, my first reaction was not one of fear

or horror. I just thought how pale and sad they all looked. . . ."

Slowly, the image faded before the visitors' eyes and finally vanished completely. Not surprisingly, the Storrers wasted no time in putting as many miles as possible between themselves and the house on the hill!

It couldn't have been a hallucination, because they had both witnessed it. Afterwards they separately recounted what they had seen, and the details tallied exactly.

It was over six months before Hans-Peter Storrer could bring himself to drive back to the village in the hills to seek an answer to the mystery that had been plaguing him. And he found it at the first place at which he called—the tiny post office run by Ludwig Wahlen.

"That house, sir, has been for sale for nearly ten years," Herr Wahlen said. "There was a shooting tragedy up there. The master shot his wife and two children. It was in all the papers."

He rummaged in a drawer and produced a yellowed sheet of newsprint. A large photograph headed the page. Looking at it, Hans-Peter saw again the sad pale faces of the dead family he had disturbed in the house on the hill.

4. THEIR MESSAGE WAS DEATH

- A lady dressed in grey—some called her "Morphine Lizzie"—visits her victims in the hospital wards.

- Dark strangers on the road bring a message of death at the moment it is taking place.

- A tall woman in white is seen only by those who are about to die.

Deadly Kindness

It was after midnight in the hospital ward. The lights were dim. A hospital ward at night can be an eerie place—one of uneasy slumber and the restless movement of people in pain.

On this night in September 1956, the women's ward at one of London's most famous hospitals was to have a most unusual visitor—a ghost on an errand of death.

The Grey Lady of St. Thomas's had visited the hospital over a dozen times since the turn of the century. On nearly every occasion, the patient who saw the apparition died soon afterwards.

On the night of September 4, 1956, the night nurse heard a gentle tapping on the outer door of the ward. It was 12:35 A.M. Around her, patients were sleeping.

In one corner, in a screened bed, an elderly woman lay gravely and, it was feared, fatally ill. The nurse had been thinking how sad it was that this old lady should die alone with no relatives or friends at her bedside. Then she heard the tapping again, louder this time.

She walked across the room and opened the door. Outside stood a woman dressed in grey. The nurse took her to be a nun.

The visitor whispered the name of the dying woman, and the nurse led her to the screened bed. Ten minutes later she looked around the screens that shrouded the corner. There was no one there—except a corpse.

The patient had died.

Puzzled, the nurse asked the night receptionist if she

had seen the visitor leave. "What visitor?" was the reply. "No one came to the wards last night."

The nurse telephoned the night porter. He told the same story: "No visitors came through the gates after 9 P.M." The nurse thought she was overtired. Perhaps she had dozed off for a minute and dreamed the incident.

But the next morning a patient on the far side of the ward caught her arm as she passed. "Wasn't it nice of the nun to come and sit with that poor soul last night?" the patient remarked.

Since then the Grey Lady has been seen at least six times. And death has followed each visit.

Who is she? She is described as middle-aged and wearing a long grey gown. Some say she is visible only from the ankles upwards—because she walks on the floor level of the wards as they were before the hospital was reconstructed.

Others think she is the ghost of a ward nurse who fell down an elevator shaft at the turn of the century. Still others believe she is the wraith of a head nurse who was found dead in her office on the top floor.

But most popular is the belief that she is the ghost of "Morphine Lizzie." Lizzie Church, a nurse at the hospital, looked after her fiancé who had been admitted after an accident, and accidentally gave him a fatal dose of morphine. Now she is said to appear whenever desperately ill patients are given morphine injections.

Most nurses have a healthy respect for hospital taboos and superstitions. Some will not put red and white flowers together in a vase. To do so, they say, means a death in the ward. And others won't allow white lilies in a patient's room. There is an old hospital belief that they too lead to death.

But not too many of St. Thomas's Hospital nurses believed in the tales of the Grey Lady until one day in 1947. Four nurses, working in the women's ward, all glanced, at various times throughout the afternoon, behind a screen that separated off a seriously ill patient. They all saw a nun and two elderly people talking to the woman.

One of the nurses told the head nurse that the patient had visitors, and the head nurse said angrily that she had not given anyone permission to be there.

She went to the ward and found the patient dead, a peaceful smile on her lips—and no sign of visitors.

Later one of the nurses going through the dead woman's effects with a relative saw a small gold locket. Inside were two photographs of a couple she instantly recognized. They were the elderly people she had seen with the nun.

"But that's not possible," said the mystified relation. "They are her father and mother—they both died years ago."

On another occasion, a patient in a men's ward at St. Thomas's looked up surprised as the young night nurse picked up his water jug. "There's no need to fill it, nurse," he said. "That nice lady in grey has just given me a glass of water." The man pointed to the foot of the bed. The nurse looked but there was no one there. She did not argue. She knew what happened to people who claimed to see the ghost dressed in grey.

The patient, not seriously ill, took a sudden and inexplicable turn for the worse.

He died the next day, 24 hours to the minute after the Grey Lady had offered her deadly kindness.

The Dark Strangers Who Told of Death

One summer afternoon in the middle of the last century, a group of boys left St. Edmund's College, a well known school about 40 miles north of London, for a boat ride.

The outing, which began as a happy outing, was to end in grim tragedy. One of the boys, Philip Weld, was to die in a whirlpool in the River Lea—and by some mysterious and inexplicable process, his father, over 200 miles away, was to learn of the death at that very moment from two strangers he met on the road.

There were 15 boys in the group, and they left school shortly after lunch. At about 5 P.M., Philip was rowing a skiff containing three others when they decided to change places. A boy named Joseph Barron was to get his turn at the oars.

Philip stood up and edged his way to the bow, while Joseph took his place. Suddenly, an unseen current seized the boat and swung it violently to the left. Philip clung to the side of the boat, lost his balance and fell into the river.

Cries of alarm turned to shouts of laughter as Philip reappeared—the water was only up to his waist. Joseph moved the boat over and the other two boys prepared to drag Philip aboard.

As they reached out, there was a swirl of water and a cry. Philip disappeared before their eyes!

The alarm was raised and other boats arrived on the

scene. They discovered that Weld had been standing on a thick shelf of clay that had given way under his weight and dragged him down to the river bottom.

The teacher in charge sent the students home and contacted the president of the college, Dr. James Cox. Workmen with grappling hooks were called out, but they failed to locate the body. Although recovery operations went on until dark, nothing was found.

The next day, a lock farther downstream was opened, and the movement of the water dislodged the body from its clay tomb.

Dr. Cox did not return to St. Edmund's but travelled to London and from there to Southampton to tell Philip Weld's father of the tragedy personally. With a priest, the Rev. Joseph Siddons, he went to Weld's home and saw the dead boy's father walking near the house.

The two men left their carriage and walked towards James Weld. As they approached, Weld said: "You need not say one word, gentlemen. I know my son is dead."

Then he told a strange story. The previous afternoon he had been walking with his daughter along a lane near his house when he suddenly saw his son Philip. The boy was standing on the opposite side of the road between two men dressed in black robes.

The daughter exclaimed, "Look—have you ever seen anyone looking so much like Philip?"

Her father replied: "It must be him—it can be no one else."

They noticed as they hurried towards the group that Philip was laughing and talking to the smaller of his companions. Suddenly, all three vanished!

James Weld, certain that the vision signified some impending disaster, went directly home. When the mail arrived, he scanned it with dread, expecting some bad news of his son. But there were only the usual bills and invitations.

"But when I saw you in a carriage outside my gate, I knew without doubt what you had come to tell me."

Dr. Cox asked Mr. Weld if he had ever seen the men in the black robes before. He said that he had not, but the faces were so indelibly impressed on his mind that he would instantly know them again.

Dr. Cox then told Mr. Weld of the circumstances of Philip's death—which took place at the very time the vision had appeared.

At the funeral, the father scrutinized all the people who came to pay their last respects to Philip, but the men in the black robes were not among them.

Months passed, and James Weld took his family on vacation in Lancashire.

One Sunday, after attending the evening service at the local church, James Weld called on the priest, Father Charles Raby.

As he waited in the parlor, Weld glanced at the framed portraits on the wall. One, unnamed, pulled him up with a start. The features, the set of the jaw, the shape of the head—he had seen them all before; he knew them as well as he knew his own face. It was the man who had been at his son's side the day he saw him in the lane.

He asked Father Raby about the portrait. He was told it was of St. Stanislaus, a Jesuit saint—the patron saint of drowning men.

The White Lady's Reign of Death

Three people in the village of Bryanston, near Blandford in Dorset, saw the Lady in White during that long, hot summer, and they lived but briefly to tell the tale.

No one knew whether the Lady in White was real or not; it's doubtful if they ever will. One thing they did know for certain was that she was the harbinger of death.

Early in May, at dusk, farm worker Robert Crewe was walking home when a tall woman dressed in white stopped him in a narrow lane.

"I am looking for the house of Robert Crewe," she told him. "I have a message for him."

"Then you're in luck," he replied, "for I am the man."

"As I said that," Crewe told his wife later, "the lane seemed to suddenly grow dark and the woman disappeared."

Three days later, Robert Crewe was kicked to death by a horse he was grooming in a stable, and the White Lady's reign of terror had begun.

John Allen, a keeper on an estate near Blandford, spent most of that summer with two other men cutting weeds in the River Stour. He was a cheerful and kindly man, but one night in July he came home from his work and cried bitterly for more than an hour.

His wife, trying to comfort him, asked what was the matter and Allen replied that he had seen a sign that made him sure he didn't have long to live. He refused to say what he had seen, but remained in low spirits for the rest of the week. He went to work as usual the next day and nothing happened. Eventually, thinking he had been mistaken, he regained some of his good humor and life in the Allen family returned to normal.

The Allens had two daughters, Mary, aged six, and Polly, three. At the beginning of August, Polly had been playing in the front yard when she ran in with some strange news.

"There was a tall lady in a white dress coming down the hill opposite," she said. "She asked me where my father was and I said he was at the river."

Curious to know who the stranger was, Mrs. Allen went out front. There was no one there. The road leading to the village was empty. Mrs. Allen remarked to her sister, who had come for tea, "Polly must have imagined it—whoever saw a woman dressed in white in these parts on a workday?"

But the child insisted that she had been spoken to by a woman who was "terribly tall, much taller than you, Mother."

As Polly went out to play, Mrs. Allen glanced at the clock. It was 4 P.M. She put on the kettle and set the table for tea. At that precise moment, the body of John Allen was floating lifelessly in the River Stour.

With two companions named Elforde and Ball, he had been standing in the river cutting weeds from the bank when he slipped and fell into a deep, mud-filled hole in the river bed. By the time his companions found his body, John Allen was dead.

They took the body to a nearby church and the priest broke the news to Allen's family.

When told of her husband's death, Mrs. Allen immediately said to her sister: "That must have been poor John's spirit that Polly saw."

The rest of the village did not agree with this view. They were convinced the apparition was the White Lady, the malevolent being who brought death to all who saw her.

Their conviction was certainly strengthened when, on September 4, Polly Allen was fatally injured by the moving wheels of a farm cart, into which she ran while playing in the village street.

5. JINXED!

- Can a car be evil?

- Can an encounter with a ghostly ship—bathed in a strange red light—spell disaster for any ship whose bow she crosses?

- Is it possible that a ring can carry a curse to all who own it?

The Car with Murder in Its Heart

The dark green open touring car with bright emerald upholstery rolled out of its garage into the June sunshine, and Franz, Count Harrach, contemplated it with an anxious frown.

It was the newest, most expensive car in the city of Sarajevo, in Serbia (now Yugoslavia). It was to be used that day to take the Archduke Franz Ferdinand, heir to the throne of Austria, on a tour of welcome through the city.

And yet, the car, a 1912 Graf and Sift, had a reputation. It was the central figure in a series of bizarre accidents. Disaster struck many of those who came in contact with it.

A year before, in the summer of 1913, Count Harrach's chauffeur mowed down two peasants in a lane outside Sarajevo, killing both of them and seriously injuring himself.

Six months later, the car was involved in another accident in which a young nobleman lost his right arm. Was it coincidence? Eventually, the Count convinced himself that it was. He permitted the Archduke to ride in the Graf and Sift through the streets of Sarajevo—and fall victim to a murderer's bullet, in an assassination that was to plunge the world into war.

It was on a Sunday, June 28, 1914, that the Archduke and his wife entered Sarajevo. The sun was shining, the crowd was friendly. The threat of violence seemed remote indeed.

The Graf and Sift was second in the motorcade. The Archduke sat in the left rear seat with his wife beside him. Next to them, on folding seats, sat the Governor of Bosnia and Count Harrach.

As the procession approached the City Council Chamber, a young anarchist named Nedjelko Cabrinovik threw a homemade bomb into the royal car. The bomb landed on the rolled-up hood.

Instantly, Archduke Ferdinand wheeled around and swept the device into the road. The car lurched forward as the driver jammed down the accelerator.

But the jinxed car was not yet finished with the Archduke.

Five minutes later, another assassin, Vagrilo Princip, pushed his way through the crowd, raised a pistol and shot Ferdinand through the throat. A second shot burst through the side of the car and seriously wounded the Archduchess.

They were two of the most fateful shots in history. A month later, Austria declared war on Serbia. Russia came to the aid of Serbia, Germany sided with Austria, and within six weeks of the murder, the whole of Europe was at war.

Count Harrach became an officer in the Serbian Army and used the Graf and Sift as his staff car. Three officers carried in it were killed in an ambush. The car spent the rest of the war in a farmyard.

Afterwards, it carried on a war of its own. It was sold to a Serbian government official who, one day in 1919, collided with a train at a level crossing. The official was thrown out and killed. The car was undamaged.

The driver's relatives ordered the jinxed car to be demolished, but a doctor asked to be allowed to buy it. He was crushed to death when it overturned.

A Swiss racing driver became the next ill-fated owner. He had it completely rebuilt and modified, and entered it for a French Automobile Club race in Orleans. In third place, the car suddenly veered off the road and came to rest in a ditch. As usual, it was undamaged, but the driver was dead. A medical examination revealed that he had died of a heart attack.

A farmer near Paris became the next owner and used the car without incident for nearly two years. One morning, he was about to leave for the market when the vehicle stalled and refused to restart. It roared into life after a tow from a tractor.

As the farmer walked around to the front of the vehicle, it unaccountably slipped into gear, jerked forward and ran its owner down.

Once again it was sold. Once again it was bought by a

man who scoffed at the idea of a car being jinxed. The new owner had the bodywork modified and the color changed to black. But the car still had murder in its heart.

It claimed five more victims—four passengers and the new owner—before it was locked in a garage in Strasbourg. So lurid was its reputation that no wrecker would attempt to dismantle it.

The job was finally done by Allied bombers in World War II and the curse of the Graf and Sift was broken at last.

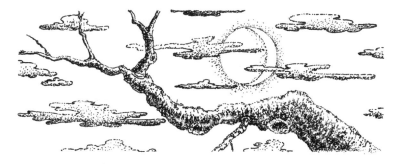

The Jinx Ship

Heading a squadron of British men-of-war, the ship called the *Bacchante*, homeward bound from Australia to England, foamed through the Pacific swell on an early June day in 1881. Smoke poured from her high stacks; she was in a hurry to get home after an extensive tour of Far East duty.

Suddenly, amid a clamor of engine-room bells, the great ship's speed began to slacken. Officers on the bridge turned their binoculars westward, and men hurried to the starboard rail.

For, standing in stark relief near the horizon, was a sailing ship on fire.

Or was it on fire? Rather, the vessel was bathed in a strange red light. Two other warships in the squadron, the *Cleopatra* and the *Tourmaline*, flashed signals to the *Bacchante* asking about the "strange glow."

The sailing ship came to within 200 yards of the *Bacchante* and sailed serenely across her bows. As she turned, the name on her stern could be seen clearly. She was the *Libera Nos*, ghost ship of the Pacific.

A murmur of consternation ran through the *Bacchante's* crew. Quickly Captain George Francis rang for full speed, and instructed his men to get back to their duties. It was a time when every man needed his mind fully occupied. They all knew what it meant for the *Libera Nos* to cross a vessel's bows: Disaster and tragedy would inevitably follow.

Legends had quickly woven themselves around the disappearance of the brig ten years earlier. It was said that her master, Captain Bernard Fokke, in order to make port in record time, had gambled with the devil and lost.

Since that day, the "ship of death" with a crew of skeletons sailed the Pacific sending ships to their doom.

Some sailors had claimed to have seen a skeleton captain standing on the fo'c'sle head holding a telescope and an hourglass.

The traditions of the British Navy made no concessions to mystery and sea lore. The day's entry in the log of the *Bacchante*, in its usual matter-of-fact phrasing, serves only to make more bizarre the facts it contains:

"There is no doubt that a ship bathed in a strange red glow did approach us. Our lookout man on the forecastle reported her as close to our starboard bow, where also the officer of the watch on the bridge clearly saw her.

"At least 100 persons saw her, yet soon after she had crossed our bows and her name had become visible, she appeared to vanish.

"There was no vestige nor any sign of any material ship to be seen either near, or away to, the horizon. Whether it was the *Libera Nos* or one of the other alleged phantom ships which are claimed to haunt the area must remain unknown.

"During the forenoon watch, the seaman who had first reported the phantom vessel fell from our foremast crosstrees and was killed instantly. He was a smart seaman, one of the most promising hands in the ship, and every man on board feels sad and despondent at his loss."

That was not the end. When the squadron reached port, the commander was stricken with a fatal illness, and the *Cleopatra* was badly damaged while docking.

The *Libera Nos* was seen again in 1893 by a clipper bound for New Zealand. Two years later, a homeward-bound Australian captain logged her as "painted bright yellow, three-masted, and what sails she wore hung tattered from square yards."

In 1899 the steamship *Hannah Regan*, bound for Europe with over a million dollars' worth of gold, lost her propellers and was badly damaged in heavy weather. She sank in deep water near Okinawa. Her log, with the bodies of the captain, first mate, and four of her crew, drifted ashore in an open boat some weeks later.

The log referred to a "phantom brig, bathed in a red-gold glow." Ominously, that was the last entry.

Salvage operations were planned. An ocean-going tug sailed from San Francisco and located the wreck. That evening, the captain of the tug was strolling around his deck when he noticed a shadow about half a mile out to sea.

"Slowly the shadow assumed the shape and appearance of a sailing vessel. She was heading in our direction and driving along as if in the grip of violent winds, although there was no wind and the sea was flat calm.

"She came right alongside and I doubted my own shocked senses, for I could see right through her, though every detail of her deck work and rigging stood out clearly. As I watched, she sank slowly beneath the sea and disappeared."

The salvage crew assembled shortly after dawn the next day and got to work. Two divers went down into the wreck—and never emerged alive. Both were found dead with their air-pipes severed. There was no rational explanation for the tragedy.

The salvage attempt met with so many mishaps that it was eventually abandoned, leaving all that was left of the *Hannah Regan* and her cargo of gold to be torn apart by the sea.

But the ship of death sailed on. During World War II, German U-boat crews claimed to have seen the phantom while on tours of duty east of Suez. Some asked for a transfer to Atlantic duty rather than run the risk of seeing the ghost ship again.

And every one of the U-boats that encountered the *Libera Nos* was lost on subsequent missions.

The Valentino Ring

In the vault of a Los Angeles bank lies a silver ring set with a semiprecious stone. It is not a particularly pretty ring or even a very valuable one, and chances are that no one will ever dare to wear it again. It lies in the vault because it bears one of the most malignant curses in the history of the occult. Successive owners have suffered injury, misfortune, even death.

And many people still believe that it was this ring that sent Rudolph Valentino to a premature grave.

Certainly, the violent incidents that have surrounded it over the past 60 years can hardly be shrugged off as mere coincidences.

It was in 1920 that Valentino, at the peak of his success, saw the ring in a San Francisco jeweller's. The proprietor warned him that the ring was a jinx, but Valentino still bought it.

He wore the ring in his next picture, *The Young Rajah*. It was the biggest flop of his career and he was off the screen for the next two years.

He did not wear the ring again until he used it as a costume prop in *The Son of the Sheik*. Three weeks after finishing this film, he went to New York on vacation.

While wearing the ring, he suffered an acute attack of appendicitis. Two weeks later, he was dead.

Pola Negri, a famous female movie star of the time, asked to pick a memento from Valentino's possessions, chose the ring—and almost immediately suffered a long period of ill health that threatened to end her career.

A year later, while convalescing, she met a performer who was almost Valentino's double, Russ Colombo. Miss Negri was so struck by the resemblance that she gave him Rudolph's ring, saying: "From one Valentino to another."

Within a few days of receiving the gift, Russ Colombo was killed in a freak shooting accident.

His cousin passed the ring on to Russ's best friend, Joe Casino. Also at the height of his popularity as an entertainer, Casino took no chances with the ring. Instead of wearing it, he kept it in a glass case in memory of his dead friend. When he was asked to donate it to a museum of Valentino relics, he refused, saying that he treasured it for sentimental reasons.

As time passed, Joe Casino forgot the ring's evil reputation and put it on. A week later, still wearing the ring, he was knocked down by a truck and killed.

By now the curse was front-page news. When asked what he proposed to do with the ring, Joe's brother, Del, explained that he could not allow himself to be intimidated by a curse or jinx or ghost or whatever it was. He didn't believe in things like that.

Del Casino wore the ring for some time and nothing unusual happened. Then he lent it to a collector of Valentino relics, who suffered no ill effects either. This caused several newspapers to speculate that at last the evil influence of the ring had come to an end. And that seemed to trigger off a new wave of violence.

One night soon afterwards, the home of Del Casino

was burgled. The police saw the burglar, a man named James Willis, running from the scene. One of them fired a warning shot, but the bullet went low and killed Willis. Among the loot found in his possession was the Valentino ring.

It was at this time that Hollywood producer Edward Small decided to make a film based on Valentino's career.

Jack Dunn, a former skating partner to ice star Sonja Henie, bore a great resemblance to Rudolph and was asked to make a film test for the part. He dressed in Valentino's clothes for the test—and also wore the jinxed ring.

Only 21 years old at the time, Dunn died 10 days later from a rare blood disease.

After this tragedy the ring was kept out of sight and never worn by anyone again, but that did not seem to curb its fatal influence.

A year after Jack Dunn's death, a daring raid was carried out in broad daylight on a Los Angeles bank in which thieves got away with a haul of over $200,000. In a subsequent police ambush, two of the gang were caught and three passers-by seriously injured. The leader of the bank robbers, Alfred Hahn, was jailed for life.

At his trial, Hahn remarked: "If I'd known what was in that vault apart from money, I'd have picked myself another bank."

For in the bank's safe deposit vault was the Valentino ring.

Can an inanimate object exert a malign influence on those who come into contact with it? All those who have, over the years, suffered the jinx of Valentino's ring have little doubt that it can. And who can blame them?

6. THERE IS SUCH A THING AS EVIL

- Evil exists—on the chalky cliffs above the English Channel.

- It lurks in a country cottage where an ordinary family is attacked by "The Thing."

- It thrives on a beautiful tropical island where natives call on a murderous spirit for revenge.

Evil on the Cliffs

The chalk cliffs of Beachy Head tower nearly 600 feet above the grey water of the English Channel. It is the loftiest headland in southern England, a lonely spot in Sussex in which few people care to loiter. For Beachy Head has a grim history and a macabre reputation.

High among the chalk crags, where the wind always howls even on the balmiest summer day, dwells the most malevolent spirit in Britain. It is an evil influence that, it is claimed, has, in the past 20 years, hurled more than 100 victims over the edge to their deaths on the cruel wave-lashed rocks below.

Many people have stated positively—some under oath—that they have felt the evil influence on the cliffs. They claim they had to combat violently a power that attempted to force them over the edge to their doom.

Few can stand near the edge of Beachy Head without being aware that some almost hypnotic power lurks in its towering cliffs. A few years ago, a young girl stumbled back hysterically from the Head and up to a patrolling policeman. She said that while she was resting on the cliffs, a dark shadow suddenly descended around her. She said she felt herself in a strange, dank atmosphere—even though the sun was shining brightly at the time.

She got up and began to run, and "some huge menacing form seemed to follow me, driving me towards the edge of the cliffs." Screaming for help, she turned and ran away from the cliffs—to safety.

The belief that there is an evil influence luring people to hurl themselves over the cliffs of Beachy Head has been common gossip in Sussex for at least four centuries. Local people agree that the cliffs have a strange and menacing atmosphere. "The soft deceptive chalk seems always waiting to hurl you headlong downwards," says a local fisherman.

The influence of the mysterious power extends even beyond the cliffs. A nearby manor house has for centuries been visited regularly by disaster and plagues that have from time to time killed off scores of animals and even taken their toll of human life.

In fact, it is from this house that the trouble is said to stem. When Britain's monasteries were dissolved in 1538, monks from a nearby abbey took refuge in the manor. The story goes that the owner of the manor betrayed their hiding place. The monks were said to have laid a curse on the man, his family and his possessions.

This, say the local people, is the cause of the malevolence that lurks on the cliffs and in the surrounding districts.

For centuries, people in the district had left the phenomenon alone. But in 1952 a group of people gathered on the cliff top intending to exorcise the evil spirit once and for all.

About 100 people accompanied medium Ray de Vekey to the top of Beachy Head on a wild night in February. By the light of pressure lamps, they gathered to try to contact the spirits of some of the people who had committed suicide there. But then, in a macabre scene unprecedented in occult research, the medium was suddenly attacked by a presence that urged him to jump over the cliff himself.

De Vekey said afterwards that the spirit was fully visible to him. It was an elderly bearded man wearing an ankle-length robe like a monk's habit, with black marking on the back.

"It was in chains," said the medium. "Not handcuffs, but ancient wrought-iron shackles. I don't think anyone could have jumped from the cliffs in chains like that. I imagine it was the spirit of someone who had been bound and thrown from the cliffs centuries ago."

The seance began in the ordinary way, with de Vekey calling on the spirit to make some sign he could recognize.

Suddenly he walked towards the edge of the cliff out of the light of the lamps. The watchers moved forward in alarm.

They heard de Vekey shout: "There is a voice calling 'Oh Helen.' There is a George Foster being called." Then, "Peggy Jordan destroyed herself here. . . ."

"There is a bearded man," de Vekey continued, his voice rising above the wind. "He is evil. He is calling us a lot of blaspheming fools. He is saying he will sweep us all over. . . ."

The medium began to laugh wildly. Four people rushed forward to restrain him from hurling himself over the cliff edge. Apparently possessed, he struggled desperately with his rescuers.

"This thing wants revenge," he shouted. "He wants his own back. He has lain in wait for years." His struggles became more violent; then suddenly de Vekey went limp and was dragged back to safety.

After the seance, de Vekey explained: "This was the strongest influence I have ever encountered. I seemed impelled towards the cliff edge. The spectre was of someone who was chained, perhaps the victim of a sacrifice, who has hated and wished ill to all ever since."

A week later, the group again climbed the cliff and de Vekey said prayers. This time nothing unusual happened. The medium said: "I think the unquiet spirit has been laid to rest forever."

But has it? Several years later, two climbers claimed they felt a "malign presence" hovering over them as they walked along the downs behind Beachy Head. Is the mysterious evil thing that lurks high above the sea gathering strength to claim more victims?

The Strangling Hands

The phantom hands clamped around the child's face, and the room was filled with the chill of death. William Bayles, standing over his daughter's cot, could see the dents in her flesh made by the force of the invisible fingers.

William Bayles and his family had for weeks been terrorized by a presence they called "The Thing," a malignant being that had transformed their cottage near West Auckland, in England's County Durham, into a house of fear. It was in the spring of 1953 that The Thing first arrived at the cottage, where Mr. Bayles, a 40-year-old garage owner, lived with his wife and young daughter.

First it lurked outside. "We heard a shuffling out in

the garden," Mr. Bayles later told investigators. "This occurred for some nights, and then gradually The Thing seemed to nose its way into the house and become mixed up with our lives."

The Bayleses were not easily frightened, but the presence that infiltrated their home filled them with bewilderment and finally with terror. Eventually its presence made itself felt every night.

The family couldn't sleep. Furniture was moved, clothes and books disturbed. One night Mr. Bayles's wife Lottie was grabbed by unseen hands and pulled across the room. Often when the family retired for the night, they found the beds were warm—as though something had already been lying on them.

The family cat refused to remain in the house at night. Mysterious knocks and clatters disturbed even the most sound sleeper.

The final horror came one night when the Bayles's young daughter, Doreen, was asleep in her cot in her parents' room. Mr. Bayles later described in detail a scene he would never forget:

"First we felt The Thing arrive in the usual way. Everything became chilled and there was a peculiar odor, the smell of a decaying jungle. Then I noticed that Doreen had begun to struggle in her sleep. As we watched, one of Doreen's eyes was forced open and then the other. It was as if someone was forcing them open with a thumb and forefinger. We could see the marks of the fingers on her skin.

"Lottie and I clung to each other terrified. Then I forced myself to go over to the cot and pry the hands away. I am sure they meant to murder the child.

"I swept my fist over Doreen's face and at once her head fell back onto the pillow, her eyes closed, and her skin resumed its natural folds."

But there was no sleep for Lottie and William Bayles that night. As the dawn was breaking, they vowed that they had suffered enough. If The Thing wanted them to leave their home, they would.

By now, the haunted cottage had become famous. A group of psychic investigators, intrigued by the reports, asked whether they could spend a few days at the place. The Bayles family agreed. They had already found another home and wanted nothing more to do with the cottage.

In June, 1953, two men, equipped with tape recorders and infrared cameras, installed themselves in the haunted room. They locked the door and waited.

A report compiled the next day reads as follows: "We both fell asleep but were awakened by the sound of something soft plopping about on the floor outside the door. There was a silence and then a pawing sound at the bottom of the door.

"We opened the door and dashed out onto the landing. Our flashlights revealed a curious green haze which drifted eerily near the ceiling. We were conscious of a horrible smell, a smell of decay and rottenness.

"We returned to the room and locked the door. We both had the impression that someone—or something—was on watch outside the door the whole night. With the first light the gaseous smell disappeared and the fumbling sounds went away.

"This convinced us that the watcher on our threshold

was a creature of darkness and could not face the clean morning air."

The investigators left the cottage none the wiser. It was left to a surveyor and archaeologist to advance the most reasonable explanation of The Thing.

He suggested that the cottage was built over an ancient well that, under certain conditions, gave out a pungent gas that drifted through the floor of the cottage. As it moved, it disturbed the foundations, creating both the smell and the noises.

But why did they disappear at dawn? How do you explain the episode of the "phantom hands"? How were furniture and belongings physically moved?

These are questions no one can answer. The tale of "The Thing" remains a classic example of the inexplicable—stranger, indeed, than fiction.

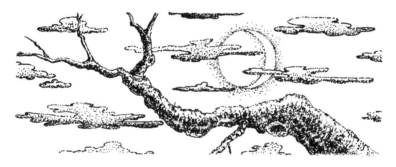

The Deadly Spirit of Raku-nene

The hot afternoon sun was blazing down on the tropical Gilbert Islands that straddle the Equator in the Pacific Ocean. It was 1917, and the war in Europe was grinding hopelessly on, but here all was peaceful.

In his thatched office in the central island of Abemama sat the district officer of the British colonial service, Arthur Grimble. Grimble, a thin, studious man, lifted his head in bewilderment as a high-pitched, wavering cry came floating over the palms. It went on and on— the cry of somebody with seemingly endless breath.

The district officer left his hut and walked slowly through clumps of trees towards the sound. Eventually, he reached the leaf hut of a native constable—and sitting outside the dwelling he saw a young woman. She was wailing mournfully, but not in anger or pain. Her eyes were staring into space.

He didn't know it then, but Arthur Grimble was looking at a girl who was under a spell of death.

She was only about 17, and obviously in the grip of some mysterious and serious disease. She had become ill, her policeman father told Grimble, at about dawn that day.

When Grimble asked why he wasn't doing anything to help the girl, he was astounded to hear the native reply: "It would be of no use. She is dying. She is being killed by the evil spirit Raku-nene."

Why, the British officer demanded, should the girl have been put under a spell of death? The answer was simple—she had scorned a man who loved her, and he had asked Raku-nene to wreak revenge for him.

Grimble angrily brushed the girl's family aside and dragged her into the hut. There he gave her a sedative. The girl's brother looked on sadly and said: "You waste your time. You cannot fight a spirit with your white powers."

Grimble made the girl as comfortable as he could, but she continued moaning loudly. He demanded to see the lover who had ordered the spirit Raku-nene to put the girl under a death spell.

When he met him, he was surprised to hear the young man admit: "Yes, she scorned me and must pay the penalty. I took a strand of her hair and tied it around my thigh for three days. Then I burned it and called on Raku-nene. This is how it is done."

That night, as the girl lay moaning, her father and brother and other family friends approached her to try to calm her. She seized a knife and attacked them with it, shrieking that she wanted to be left alone. They left her alone and she died the next day. Just before dying she screamed the word, "Raku-nene," over and over.

Arthur Grimble went to the family hut and examined her body. He found no trace of disease and no injuries. His official report was that she died of natural causes.

Grimble dismissed the unhappy affair from his mind, but two years later he had cause to remember it: Another woman died in similar circumstances. After her death Grimble spoke to a man he knew had been friendly with her.

The man told him: "She rejected me—she found another. So I called on Raku-nene, as is our custom."

Auto-suggestion? Hypnosis? Grimble found no evidence of either. In fact, the man in this incident told Grimble that he had not informed the woman that he had called on the spirit Raku-nene to place a spell on her.

Again, Grimble found on examination that death appeared due to natural causes.

Later, the British administration learned of so many deaths among Gilbert Island women with no sound reason for them that they ordered penal servitude for anybody found guilty of Raku-nene magic.

Grimble was unwilling to accept the fact that an evil spirit could cause the death of a human being. But he did admit: "There is among the island women a sudden form of madness accompanied by physical disfigurement which, in the mind of the victim, is invariably associated with the name Raku-nene."

7. DO NOT DISTURB!

- An outraged witch wreaks vengeance on a town when her tombstone is moved.

- Sudden death befalls every person present at the opening of a family vault.

- Weird violence follows the remains of the Princess of Amen-Ra in her exquisitely fashioned mummycase. Could she have been responsible for the sinking of the *Titanic*?

The Angry Witch of Scrapfaggot Green

All day long the convoys of military trucks groaned through England's east coast villages on their way to the sea. It was early in June 1944, and the Allies were massing on the Channel shores ready to make the perilous journey into France. The D-Day landings were about to begin.

The long line of American tank-carriers that had rumbled for two nights and a day eastbound from their depot, pulled up abruptly and unwillingly at Scrapfaggot Green, in the center of the sleepy village of Great Leighs.

A huge weathered stone, eight feet high and over two tons in weight, stood by the roadside, barring the way of the wide trucks. Schedules were brutally tight. The past had to stand aside while current history was made. A wire hawser lassoed the stone, and it was wrenched from its socket and dragged away.

The convoy moved on. And the village remained—to be tyrannized by the spectre whose tombstone had been displaced. For the reign of terror of the Witch of Scrapfaggot Green, has, by its unique and eerie violence, become a part of psychical folklore.

Three hundred years earlier, so the story went, the witch had been buried, with a stake through her heart, at the Scrapfaggot Green crossroads. And she had lain quietly until only a few hours after the stone's removal, when extraordinary things began to happen.

The bell in the church tower tolled in the early hours of the morning—when nobody was near it!

The following Sunday, the bells played reverse chimes—which stopped as soon as anyone entered the church!

For several days running, the church clock struck midnight—at 2:30 in the morning!

A local farmer's haystacks were pushed over during the night, and stacks of corn from one meadow were found the next morning in another.

Hens stopped laying; chickens were found drowned in water barrels.

Sheep were found in the wrong field—though their own field was locked and the hedges unbroken. Three geese owned by the landlord of a local pub disappeared from his garden overnight and were never seen again!

In a builder's yard, a pile of scaffold poles, neatly stacked, were found scattered all over. But no noise had been heard during the night!

Practically every adult in the village had a story to tell of unexplained happenings. Within a few days the village was in a state bordering on mass hysteria.

The newspapers sent reporters to investigate. Psychic experts were called in. And still the witch's ghost continued to disrupt the community.

Thirty sheep and two horses were found dead one morning.

Chickens in a yard and rabbits in a hutch mysteriously changed places. Yet the fasteners on the hutch had been undisturbed!

A big boulder, weighing 200 pounds, was found outside the front door of a pub. Where it had come from no one knew!

In the St. Anne's Castle Inn, a bedroom became haunted. The landlord, Arthur Sykes, had placed furniture carefully and tidily about the room, but next morning it was a shambles—a chest of drawers was on its side, bedclothes were strewn over the floor, a wardrobe was in a different position! Mr. Sykes tidied the room. Next morning it was a shambles again. He tidied it once more—and the same thing happened.

"I don't understand it," he said. "From the way the room was upset I should certainly have heard something happening, because I was sleeping in the next bedroom. But I heard nothing."

"There is no doubt that the village was subjected to a reign of terror," another reputable man related. "Most of what happened can't possibly be explained naturally. In broad daylight I saw a man's straight razor, opened, lying on the street. I went to pick it up and it jumped away from me.

"I tried again and the same thing happened. But it can't have been someone pulling it with a thin thread for a laugh, because it kept jumping *up and down*—it jumped about a foot into the air. Frankly, I was frightened. I left it there in case it attacked me."

It was high time, decided the villagers, that something was done.

A week after the disturbances started, a group of men and women recovered the witch's tombstone from where the soldiers put it, dragged it with a tractor, and in a midnight ceremony replaced it at the crossroads, exactly where it had been for generations.

The hauntings stopped from that moment. Great Leighs has been a peaceful village ever since. The witch of Scrapfaggot Green is, it seems, happy to be home.

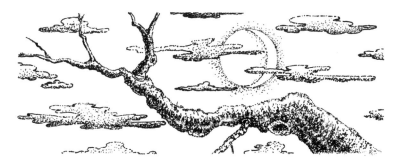

Revenge of the Stone Man

Deep under the 14th century church in the pretty English village of Cottesbrooke, 27 coffins lay in a vault. They had lain undisturbed among the musty cobwebs since the last one arrived in 1747.

Then, in 1962, the first shafts of light for over 200 years splashed down into the gloom. The vault was opened—and a curse was unleashed upon all those who peered down at the musty remains.

There were eight people around the opened tomb of the Allsop family. All of them died within the next four years—some mysteriously, others tragically—and all were said to be the victims of a ghost, Sir Joseph Allsop, the "wicked squire" of Cottesbrooke. His statue guards his burial place, unsheathed stone sword in hand. The legend was that he would not tolerate any tampering with the family vault.

And there had been no tampering—the heavy stone slabs had not been lifted for centuries—until the spring of 1962, when the parish church of St. Michael's underwent restoration. Central heating pipes needed inspection, and this meant entering the vault and moving some flagstones in its wall.

On May 24, watched by the glowering stone figure of Sir Joseph, three workmen pried up the heavy stones that marked the entrance to the vault.

It was a warm day. But everyone gathered around the tomb felt a definite chilling of the atmosphere as the stones were lifted. Two people, the churchwarden's wife,

Mrs. Mary Roper, and an elderly woman friend, felt suddenly afraid and left the church. Of all those who witnessed the scene, they are the only two still alive.

"A strange disturbing atmosphere suddenly surrounded us," Mrs. Roper explained later. "My friend felt it too. We both knew that no good would come of disturbing the sleep of the dead."

The vengeance of Sir Joseph Allsop was not long in making itself felt. The architect who supervised the restoration died suddenly in early middle age two weeks later. Three more sudden deaths followed in quick succession—a builder employed on the job, a carpenter, and a man from the surveyor's office that was supervising the work.

All the deaths were said to be from natural causes. The villagers knew differently.

The church organist, a man in his early 30s, died while halfway through a hymn at an evening service.

A 23-year-old farm worker was found lying unconscious and critically ill in a country lane. His battered bicycle lay nearby. Immediately people asked: "Has he been in the tomb?" It was found that he had. Two days later, he died.

The vault was still open and arrangements were made to have it resealed. Perhaps then the reign of terror would cease and the village would return to sleepy seclusion.

But Sir Joseph, it seemed, was not finished. Near midnight on June 19, an elderly couple walking home along a path near the churchyard heard sounds of violence coming from the church. They hurried to the village and roused the local policeman, but by the time he got to St. Michael's the noise had stopped.

The next morning, clergymen discovered that a dozen coffins had been wrenched from their niches and hurled across the floor like matchsticks in a gale.

The following day, the local grocer died. He was 41 and often boasted that he had never had a day's illness. Once again, the post mortem showed death to be due to natural causes—this time, heart failure.

The next Sunday, the tomb was sealed and reconsecrated. That, everyone hoped, would be the end of the matter.

But it was not. A spine-chilling and totally inexplicable finale brought the curtain down on the affair—an incident that was to transform an eerie ghost story to a classic tale of the unknown.

Two weeks before Christmas, 1962, Reginald Martin, the elderly sexton of St. Michael's, was found dead in the garden of his home. He was crumpled over his wheelbarrow near a compost heap. He had not been a robust man and it was assumed that the exertion of gardening had been too much for him.

Only two things, two *small* things, dashed the theory to pieces. Martin was the last survivor of the eight who had witnessed the opening of the tomb. And in his hand he grasped a tiny piece of stone.

It was an ordinary piece of stone—*but one which fitted exactly into a scar on the end of the sword that the statue of Sir Joseph Allsop held in its hand. . . .*

The Mummy's Curse

The Princess of Amen-Ra lived some 1,500 years before the birth of Christ. When she died, she was laid in an ornate wooden coffin and buried deep in a vault at Luxor, on the banks of the Nile.

Had she been left undisturbed in her vault, perhaps this would have been the end of the story. In fact, it was only the beginning. For ten years at the start of this century, the evil influence of her coffin brought death and havoc wherever it went.

Of all tales of the supernatural this one is perhaps the best documented, the most disturbing, and the most difficult to explain.

In the late 1890s, four rich young Englishmen visiting the excavations at Luxor were invited to buy an exquisitely fashioned mummy case containing the remains of the Princess of Amen-Ra.

They drew lots. The man who won paid several hundred pounds and had the coffin taken to his hotel. A few hours later he was seen walking out towards the desert. He was never seen again.

The next day, one of his companions was shot by an Egyptian servant, and wounded so severely that his arm had to be amputated.

The third man in the party found on his return home that the bank holding his entire savings had failed.

The fourth man suffered a severe illness, lost his job, and was reduced to selling matches in the street.

Eventually, the coffin reached England, where it was bought by a London businessman.

After three of his family had been injured in a road accident and his house severely damaged by fire, the owner of the coffin donated it to the British Museum.

Despite its reputation, the authorities agreed to accept the gift. But the Princess of Amen-Ra was not long in bringing calamity to her new home: As the coffin was being unloaded from a truck in the museum courtyard, the truck suddenly went into reverse, trapping a passerby who was taken to a hospital.

Then, as the casket was being lifted up the stairs by two workmen, one fell and broke his leg. The other man, in his thirties and apparently in perfect health, died unaccountably two days later.

Once the Princess was installed in the Egyptian Room, the trouble really started. Night watchmen at the museum frequently heard frantic hammering and sobbing coming from the coffin.

Other exhibits in the room were hurled about. On one occasion a keeper claimed that he had been actually attacked by a spirit who leaped out of the casket and tried to hurl him down a delivery chute with a 40-foot drop.

Cleaners at the museum refused to go near the Princess of Amen-Ra. When one man derisively flicked a dustcloth at the face painted on the coffin, his child died of measles soon afterwards.

Finally, the authorities had the mummy carried down to the basement where it could surely do no further harm.

Within a week, one of the men who had helped in the moving was seriously ill, and the supervisor of the move was found dead at his desk.

By now the papers had seized the story. A photographer took a picture of the mummy case and found when he developed it that the painting on the coffin had changed into a human—and horrifying—face. The photographer went home, locked his door and shot himself.

The museum then sold the mummy to a private collector. After continual misfortune, he banished it to the attic, where it was languishing when Madame Helena Blavatsky, a well known authority on the occult, visited the house. She did not know the history of the mummy, or that it was even on the premises. Yet as soon as she entered the house, she was seized with a shivering fit and declared there was an evil influence of incredible intensity at work.

The host, almost jokingly, invited her to have a look around. Madame Blavatsky searched the house without success, until she came to the attic and found the mummy case. She knew at once that this was the source of the evil influence she had felt.

"Can you exorcise this evil spirit?" asked the host.

"There is no such thing as exorcism," replied Madame Blavatsky. "Evil remains evil forever. Nothing can be done about it. I implore you to get rid of this evil thing as soon as possible."

The owner of the house did not take the matter seriously until a member of his family, moving some suitcases in the attic a week or so later, claimed to have seen a figure rise from the mummy case and glide across the floor. After this, he felt he should take Madame Blavatsky's advice and rid himself of the disturbing object.

No British museum would take the mummy; the fact that nearly 20 people had met with death or disaster from handling the casket was now well known.

Eventually, a hard-headed American archaeologist who dismissed the happenings as quirks of circumstance, paid a handsome price for the specimen and made arrangements for its removal to New York. In April 1912, the collector escorted his prize aboard a sparkling new White Star liner about to make its maiden voyage to New York.

On the night of April 14, amid scenes of unprecedented horror, the Princess Amen-Ra accompanied 1,500 passengers to their deaths at the bottom of the Atlantic. The name of the ship was the *Titanic*.

INDEX